TABLE OF CONTENTS

01 PRE-SHOOT CHECKLIST

Check these settings before you head out with your camera!

SETTING	MY PREFERRED SETTING
☑ Shooting Mode	....
☑ White Balance Setting	....
☑ ISO Setting	....
☑ Exposure Compensation	....
☑ Focus Mode	....
☑ Focus Method	....
☑ Drive Mode	....
☑ Metering Mode	....
☑ Picture Style	....
☑ Bracketing Setting	....
☑ Highlight Alert Setting	....
☑ File Format: JPEG/HEIF, or RAW & JPEG/HEIF	....
☑ Battery Fully Charged and In Camera	....
☑ Memory Card Formatted and In Camera	....

02 BUTTONS, DIALS, AND SCREENS

CAMERA BODY TOP

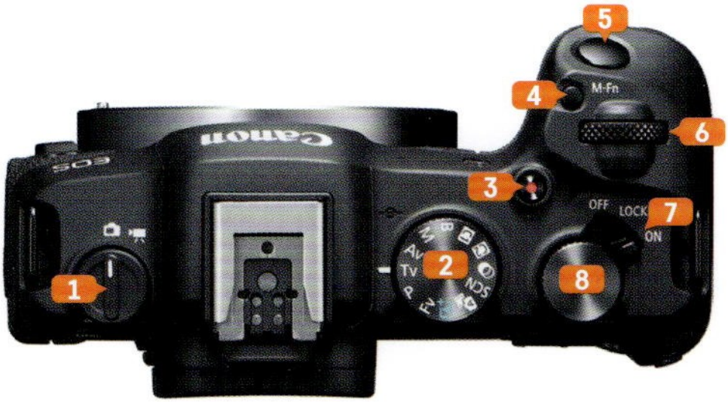

1. **Photo/Movie Switch:** Sets camera to take still images or movies.
2. **Mode Dial:** Turn to select the shooting mode.
3. **Movie Shooting Button:** Press to start/stop recording a movie.
4. **Multi-Function (M-Fn) Button:** Use this button to set WB/ Metering, Advance mode/AF mode, Flash Comp./ISO, and Picture Style/AF Area mode.
5. **Shutter Button:** Press halfway to activate autofocus; press all the way to take a photo.
6. **Main Dial:** Use this dial to set the shutter speed, aperture, and other settings.

7. Power/Lock Button: Turns the camera on or off/Lock prevents settings from being changed if you accidentally operate the Main dial, Quick Control dial, or the lens's Control Ring.

8. Quick Control Dial: Use this dial to set exposure compensation, aperture setting while in Manual Shooting mode, etc.

CAMERA BODY BACK

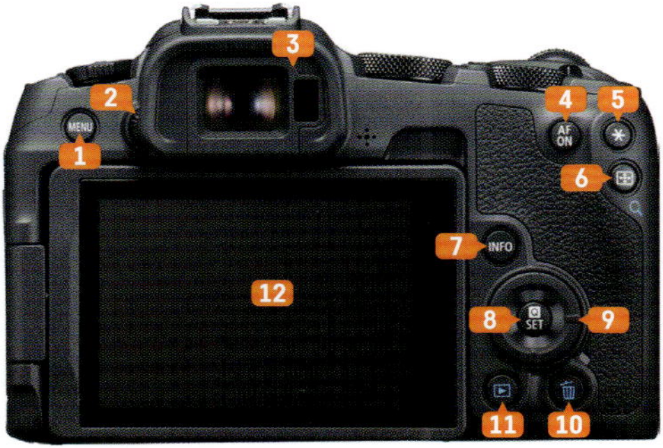

1. **MENU Button:** Press to bring up Menu options.
2. **Dioptric Adjustment Dial:** Turn to make the viewfinder display sharp.
3. **Viewfinder Sensor:** Senses when you're looking through the viewfinder and activates viewfinder display.
4. **AF Start (AF-ON) Button:** Press to engage the autofocus.
5. **AE Lock Button:** Use to lock exposure.

6. **AF Point Selection/Magnify/Reduce Button:** Use to select the desired AF-point/Use button to change view when using monitor/Use to adjust image playback options (index view, zoom in, and zoom out).
7. **INFO Button:** Press to cycle through views displaying different information.
8. **Quick Control (Q) Button/Set Button:** Use to access the Quick Control screen/Use to finalize a setting and return to a previous screen.
9. **Cross Keys:** Use to navigate menus, move focus points, etc.
10. **Erase Button:** Use to erase the current photo on display.
11. **Playback Button:** Press to view the last image taken.
12. **Screen:** Displays multiple features, options, and settings for shooting and playback.

CAMERA BODY FRONT

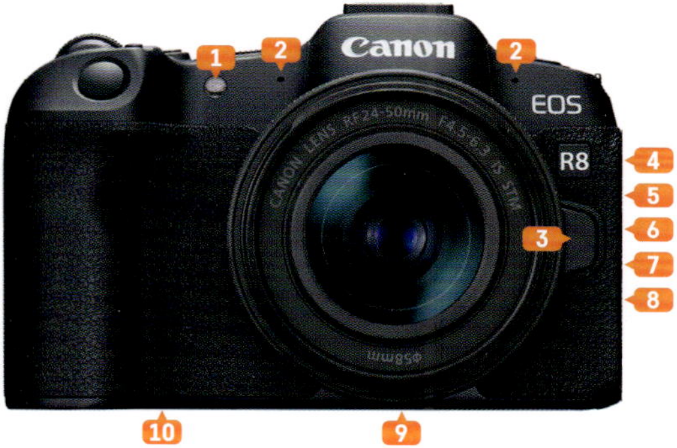

1. **AF-Assist Beam/Self-Timer/Remote Control Lamp:** Lights up area in front of camera in low light/Blinks when Self-Timer is active/Shows when remote is attached.
2. **Microphones:** Records audio when recording movies.
3. **Lens Release Button:** Press to remove lens.
4. **Remote Control Terminal:** Connect remote control to camera.
5. **HDMI Out Terminal:** Connect HDMI micro cable.
6. **Microphone Terminal:** Connect external microphone to camera.
7. **Digital Terminal:** Connect digital devices to camera.
8. **Headphones Terminal:** Connect headphones to camera.
9. **Tripod Socket (On bottom of camera):** Standard socket for tripod or monopod.
10. **Battery Compartment/Memory Card Cover (On bottom of camera):** Open to access battery compartment and memory card slot.

SHOOTING SCREEN (STILL PHOTO)

Each time you press the INFO button, the information display will change. The display will show only the settings currently applied.

Note: Viewfinder display positions will vary for some items.

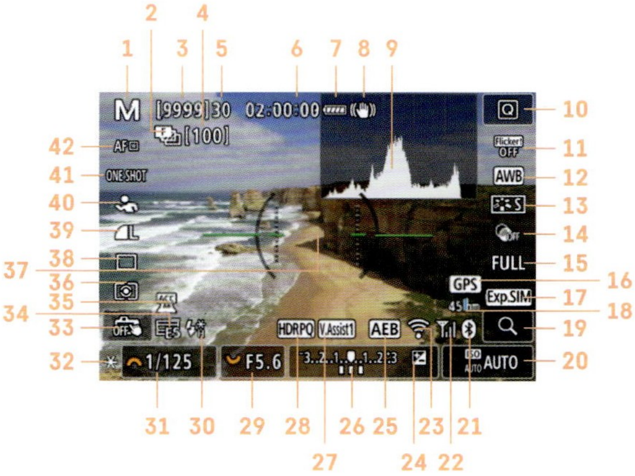

1. **Shooting Mode**
2. **Focus Bracketing/HDR/Multiple Exposures/Multi Shot Noise Reduction/Bulb Timer/Interval Timer**
3. **Possible Shots/Seconds Until Self-Timer Shoots**
4. **Number of Remaining Shots for Focus Bracketing, Multiple Exposure, or Interval Timer**

5. Maximum Burst
6. Movie Recording Time Available
7. Battery Level
8. Image Stabilizer
9. Histogram
10. Quick Control Button
11. Anti-Flicker Shooting
12. White Balance/White Balance Correction
13. Picture Style
14. Creative Filters
15. Still Photo Cropping/Aspect Ratio
16. GPS
17. Exposure Simulation
18. Focal Length
19. Magnify Button
20. ISO speed
21. Bluetooth Function
22. Wi-Fi Signal Strength
23. Wi-Fi Function
24. Exposure Compensation
25. AEB/FEB (Auto Exposure Bracketing/Flash Exposure Bracketing)
26. Exposure Level Indicator
27. View Assist
28. HDRPQ
29. Aperture Value
30. Flash Ready/FE Lock/High-Speed Sync
31. Shutter Speed
32. AE Lock (Exposure Lock)
33. Touch Shutter/Create Folder
34. Electronic Shutter
35. Accessory Attached Indicator
36. Metering Mode

37. AF Point (1-Point AF)
38. Drive Mode
39. Image Quality
40. Subject to Detect
41. AF Operation
42. AF Area

SHOOTING SCREEN (MOVIE)

Each time you press the INFO button, the information display will change. The display will show only the settings currently applied.

Note: Viewfinder display positions will vary for some items.

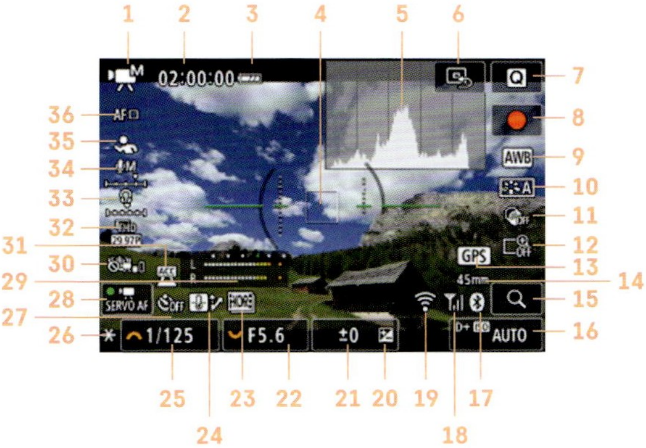

1. Movie Shooting Mode
2. Movie Recording Time Available/Elapsed Recording Time
3. Battery Level
4. AF Point (1-Point AF)
5. Histogram (Brightness/RGB)
6. Set AF Point to Center
7. Quick Control Button
8. Movie Shooting Button
9. White Balance/White Balance Correction
10. Picture Style
11. Creative Styles
12. Digital Zoom
13. GPS
14. Focal Length
15. Magnify Button
16. ISO speed
17. Bluetooth Function
18. Wi-Fi Signal Strength
19. Wi-Fi Function
20. Exposure Compensation
21. Exposure Level Indicator (Metering Levels)
22. Aperture Value
23. HDR Movie Recording
24. Overheating Warning
25. Shutter Speed
26. AE Lock
27. Movie Self-Timer
28. Movie Servo AF
29. Audio Recording Level Indicator
30. Movie Digital IS
31. Accessory Attached Indicator

32. **Movie Recording Size**
33. **Headphone Volume**
34. **Audio Recording Level (Manual Input)**
35. **Subject to Detect**
36. **AF Area**

03 ESSENTIAL MODES AND SETTINGS

SHOOTING MODES

Rotate the Mode dial to select the desired Shooting mode.

A+ (Scene Intelligent Auto): The camera assesses the scene and sets the optimum settings automatically. It will even adjust the focus on both still and moving subjects.

Fv (Flexible-Priority AE): Shutter speed, aperture, and ISO are all set automatically, then you can change one, two, or all three settings to get the desired exposure. The settings you don't change will automatically be adjusted by the camera.

P (Program AE): The camera sets the shutter speed and aperture based on metering info and current ISO.

Tv (Time Value, or Shutter Speed Priority): You set the shutter speed and the camera sets the aperture based on metering info and current ISO.

Av (Aperture Value, or Aperture Priority): You set the aperture, and the camera sets the shutter speed based on metering info and current ISO. Range of available apertures depends on the attached lens.

M (Manual): You set ISO, shutter speed, and aperture. Refer to the exposure level indicator.

Bulb: Used for long exposures. The shutter stays open as long as you hold down the shutter button. Use the Main dial to set the aperture.

C1, C2 (Custom Shooting Modes): Use the Set-Up Menu to set a custom shooting mode.

Movie: Used to record movies.

SCN (Special Scene Mode): Press the OK/Set button, use the Main dial to select the desired mode, then press OK/Set. You can pick from the following: Portrait, Group Photo, Landscape, Panoramic Shot, Sports, Kids, Panning, Close-Up, Food, Night Portrait, Handheld Night Scene, HDR Backlight Control, or Silent Shutter.

Creative Filters Mode: Press the OK/Set button, use the Main dial to select the desired mode, then press OK/Set. Choose from the following filters: Grainy Black and White, Soft Focus, Fish-eye, Water Painting, Toy Camera, Miniature, or HDR Art (Standard, Vivid, Bold, Embossed).

METERING MODES

MENU > Shooting (Screen 3) > Metering Mode

Evaluative: General-purpose mode suited for most situations and subjects (even backlit subjects).

Partial: Uses a small part of the area at the center of the screen for determining exposure. Good choice when there is very bright light around the subject.

Spot: Uses a very small area at the center of the screen. Use when you need to meter on a specific part of the scene.

Center-Weighted Average: The camera analyzes the whole scene to determine exposure, but places more emphasis on info at the center of the screen.

EXPOSURE COMPENSATION

Press the Shutter button halfway down, then rotate the Quick Control dial to adjust exposure compensation from –3 (darker) to +3 (lighter) stops, in 1/3-stop increments.

Note: The exposure compensation you set will remain in effect until you change it; it does not return to 0 when the camera is turned off.

FOCUS

MENU > AF (Screen 1) > AF Operation

Use One-Shot AF for still images and Servo AF for moving subjects. AI Focus AF automatically switches between One-Shot AF and Servo AF depending on the subject while the Shutter button is pressed.

MENU > AF (Screen 1) > AF Area

Spot AF: The camera focuses on the smallest possible area, even narrower than 1-Point AF.

1-Point AF: The camera focuses using a single point for critical focus.

Expand AF Area +: The camera uses one AF point, as well as the points above and to the left and right, to help focus. This is helpful for moving subjects that are difficult to track with 1-Point AF.

Expand AF Area: Around: The camera creates an even larger area around one AF point to find focus.

Flexible Zone AF (1, 2, or 3): The camera automatically picks the focus point using a large (square for 1, vertical for 2, horizontal for 3) area.

Whole Area AF: Camera uses the largest area to pick a focus point using information like distance and subject.

Whole Area Tracking Servo AF: When using Servo AF, you can switch to Whole Area tracking while the Shutter button is pressed halfway down. When turned on, the AF switches to Whole Area AF to try and track the subject as it moves across the frame. When turned off, the camera only uses the originally selected focus points.

Subject to Detect: MENU > AF (Screen 1) > Subject to detect. You can specify what type of subject is tracked. The choices are Auto, People, Animals, Vehicles, or None. When the Left or Right Eye is selected, the camera will try to focus on that eye first, but will switch to the other eye if needed.

Eye Detection: MENU > AF (Screen 1) > Eye Detection. Select Auto, Right Eye, or Left Eye to have the camera try to focus on the eye, or select Disable to turn it off.

Switch Between Manual and Auto Focus: MENU > AF (Screen 1) > Focus Mode.

AF turns the autofocus on, while MF lets you manually focus.

Manual Focus Peaking: MENU > AF (Screen 5) > MF Peaking Settings. When manually focusing, focus peaking informs you that focus has been achieved by lighting up when the edges of the subject are in focus.

Move the AF Point or Zone AF Frame: Press the AF Point selection button, then use the Cross Keys to move the point to the desired location. To center the AF point, press the Erase button.

DRIVE MODES

Press the M-Fn (Multi-Function) button and rotate the Control dial to select the Drive mode option, then rotate the Main dial to select the desired setting.

Single Shooting: The camera takes a single shot every time the Shutter button is fully pressed.

High-Speed Continuous Shooting: The camera takes up to 6 frames per second when you press and hold the Shutter button (approximately 20 frames per second when using the electronic shutter).

Low-Speed Continuous Shooting: The camera takes up to 3 frames per second when you press and hold the Shutter button (approximately 5 frames per second when using the electronic shutter).

Self-Timer 10: Sets the self-timer for 10 seconds.

Self-Timer 2: Sets the self-timer for 2 seconds.

Self-Timer Continuous: Shoots continuously starting in 10 seconds for the desired number of frames.

WHITE BALANCE

Press the M-Fn (Multi-Function) button and rotate the Quick Control dial to select the White Balance option, then rotate the Main dial to select the desired setting.

Auto (AWB) (Ambience Priority) setting is best for most situations. **Auto (AWB-W)** (White Priority) is best when you want to reduce a warm color cast. White balance can be set to shift colors warmer, cooler, or keep them accurate. Other settings are all matched to different lighting types. For truest colors, pick the type of lighting being used to illuminate the scene.

FILE FORMATS

MENU > Shooting (Screen 1) > Image Quality. Use the Main dial to select the RAW quality, and use the Quick Control dial to select the JPEG quality. Press Set to set the image quality.

RAW/C-RAW (Compact RAW): The RAW data from the image sensor is recorded each time a photo is taken. The C-RAW version is a compressed RAW file that takes up less space.

RAW/JPEG: If you have selected both a RAW and JPEG option, the camera saves two files each time the Shutter button is pressed: a RAW file and a JPEG file. You decide the size of the JPEG.

JPEG: The camera saves a JPEG file each time the Shutter button is pressed. You decide the size of the JPEG.

HEIF: This file type is used for HDR shooting and can be converted to JPEG after shooting.

04 OTHER HELPFUL SETTINGS

DISPLAY SIMULATION

MENU > Shooting (Screen 9) > Display Simulation. This feature displays a simulation of the current exposure settings as they are applied to the scene.

Exposure + DOF: The displayed image brightness and depth of field will be close to the actual exposure of the resulting image. Exposure compensation will change the simulated brightness of the image accordingly, as will changes to the aperture.

Exposure: The displayed image brightness will be close to the actual exposure of the resulting image. Exposure compensation will change the simulated brightness of the image accordingly.

Exposure Only During DOF Preview: Press the DOF Preview button to display image brightness and depth of field that will be close to the actual exposure of the resulting image. Exposure compensation will change the simulated brightness of the image accordingly, as will changes to the aperture.

Disable: Exposure Simulation is essentially off. The image is displayed at the standard brightness all the time, regardless of exposure settings or exposure compensation.

PICTURE STYLES

MENU > Shooting (Screen 4) > Picture Style

Allows you to adjust settings for JPEG images. Adjustable settings are Sharpness (Strength, Fineness, Threshold), Contrast, Saturation, Color Tone, Filter Effect (Monochrome), and Toning Effect (Monochrome). Eight preset picture controls can all be adjusted: **A (Auto)**, **S (Standard)**, **P (Portrait)**, **L (Landscape)**, **FD (Fine Detail)**, **N (Neutral)**, **F (Faithful)**, **M (Monochrome)**. Monochrome also has four color filters: Yellow, Orange, Red, Green. Finally, there are also three User-Defined Picture Styles, which allow you to customize any of the styles for easy access.

CUSTOM WHITE BALANCE

Setting a custom White Balance can help you get the best color when you're shooting under mixed lighting:

1. Take a photo of a white card (or white wall) under the mixed lighting at the scene (switch to Manual Focus if needed).

2. Select MENU > Shooting (Screen 4) > Custom White Balance.

3. The last photo taken will be shown (if not, select it with the Quick Control dial), and press OK.

4. Select MENU > Shooting (Screen 4) > White Balance, and select the Custom White Balance icon.

COLOR SPACE

MENU > Shooting (Screen 4) > Color Space

sRGB: Smaller color space. Best when images are used directly from camera.

Adobe RGB: Larger color space. Best used when images will be edited with post-processing software.

HIGHLIGHT ALERT (BLINKIES)

MENU > Playback (Screen 4) > Highlight Alert

Select Enable so that clipped highlights will blink, alerting you to possible overexposure when playing back images. To obtain more detail in those areas, adjust exposure settings or exposure compensation and shoot again.

NOISE REDUCTION

MENU > Shooting (Screen 5) > Long Exposure Noise Reduction

Reduces noise in images with shutter speeds of 1 second or longer. Doubles time needed to save an image to a memory card. Choices are Auto, Enable, and Disable. Auto is usually the best choice.

MENU > Shooting (Screen 5) > High ISO Speed NR

Reduces noise in images taken at high ISO settings. Use Standard for default, Low for less noise reduction, and High for more noise reduction. You can also use the Multi-Shot Noise Reduction which takes four separate images when you press the Shutter button, and merges them together into a single JPEG image. This will not work if image quality is set to RAW or RAW+JPEG.

AUTO ISO

MENU > Shooting (Screen 2) > ISO Speed Settings

Within the ISO Speed Settings, you can select Auto for the ISO Speed, then use the Auto Range option to set the minimum and maximum ISO settings to define the range that the camera can use. You can also set the Minimum Shutter Speed to ensure that the camera does not lower the shutter speed too much; this helps reduce camera shake and blurry images.

AUTO EXPOSURE BRACKETING

You can bracket a set of three exposures up to +/-3 stops in 1/3-stop increments:

1. Select MENU > Shooting (Screen 2) > Exposure Compensation/AEB.
2. Set the Bracketing range by turning the Main dial.
3. If desired, set the exposure compensation amount by using the Left and Right Cross Keys. Press Set.
4. Take the pictures, and three bracketed shots will be created. (If you're in Single shooting drive mode, take three pictures to create the bracketed sequence. If you're in a Continuous shooting drive mode, the three shots will be taken together when you press and hold the Shutter button.)

WIRELESS CONNECTION

Install the Camera Connect app on your smartphone and pair it with the EOS R8.

This will allow you to view and transfer images to your smartphone, see the Live View image on your smartphone, and even shoot remotely from your smartphone. You will need to turn smartphone Bluetooth and Wi-Fi on, and you have to use the Camera Connect app to pair the phone and the camera. When your smartphone and the camera are connected, you can browse, delete, and rate images, they can be transferred and saved on the device, remote live shooting is possible, and you can set up auto transfer of images.

RESET CAMERA

MENU > Set-Up (Screen 5) > Reset Camera

You can choose to reset Basic settings or Other settings here. The Basic settings reset restores the default for the shooting functions and menu settings while the Other settings reset restores the settings for the individual selected items.

MULTIPLE EXPOSURES

Create in-camera multiple exposures:

1. Select MENU > Shooting (Screen 6) > Multiple Exposure.

2. Select Enable to start or Disable to end multiple exposure shooting.

3. Choose a Multiple Exposure Control option:

   Additive: The exposure of each image is added cumulatively.

   Average: Based on the number of exposures you set (next step), negative exposure compensation is added automatically as you shoot to achieve a standard overall exposure.

   Bright: Retains brightest portion of images.

   Dark: Retains darkest portion of images.

4. Set the number of exposures you'd like to combine. Then press Set.

5. Specify whether you'd like to save all the individual images or just the resulting multiple exposure.

6. Set a Continue Multiple Exposure option:

1-Shot Only: Shoot just one multiple exposure.

Continuously: Continue shooting multiple exposures until you disable the feature.

7. Shoot the first image. The preview will be shown on the screen and the Multiple Exposure icon will blink.

8. Shoot the rest of the images. The exposures will combine into one image.

HDR HDR

Combine multiple images into a single JPEG/HEIF file to reduce the contrast and improve tonal range.

1. Select MENU > Shooting (Screen 2) > HDR Shooting HDR PQ.

2. Enable or disable the HDR PQ setting, which applies the PQ gamma curve to the image.

3. Select MENU > Shooting (Screen 2) > HDR Mode.

4. Select Moving Subject, Dynamic Range, or Off (to return to normal shooting).

5. When using Moving Subject mode, the camera automatically combines images to keep the subject in focus and give the widest tone range. You can Limit max brightness for playback when using a monitor exceeding 1000 nits—only available when HDR shooting PQ mode is enabled.

6. When you choose the dynamic range, you can then set the following:

Dynamic Range: Auto: Sets the dynamic range automatically depending on the scene's tonal range, or you can elect a value (the higher the number, the wider the dynamic range).

Limit max brightness: When HDR PQ is enabled, you can limit the brightness so the image displays correctly on monitors brighter than 1000 nits.

Continuous HDR: 1 Shot Only: You'll only shoot one HDR image.

Every Shot: You'll keep shooting HDR images until you disable HDR shooting by selecting Disable HDR (see steps 3 and 4).

7. Select the Auto Image Align setting:

Enable: Choose this if you're shooting handheld.

Disable: Choose this if you're shooting on a tripod.

Save Source Images: Determine if you'd like to save all the images that you shoot or just the resulting HDR image.

8. Take the picture.

TIME-LAPSE MOVIES

Create a time-lapse movie in-camera:

1. Select MENU > Shooting (Screen 6) > Time-Lapse Movie.
2. Select an Interval between 2 seconds and 99:59.59. You can see both the time required and the playback time on the display.

3. Set the Number of Shots you'd like to take for the time-lapse movie (2–3600).

4. Select the desired movie recording size (4k or Full HD).

5. Select Auto Exposure to choose the shooting method:

Fixed 1st Frame: The first shot is metered, then all subsequent shots match that first shot's exposure.

Each Frame: Each frame is metered and shot separately.

6. In the Screen Auto Off option, choose Disable to have the image displayed (though the screen will automatically turn off 30 minutes after the time-lapse shooting begins); choose Enable to have the screen turn off 10 seconds after the time-lapse shooting begins.

Note: You can press the INFO button at any time during time-lapse shooting to turn the screen on or off.

7. Choose whether you'd like to hear a beep after every image is captured (Beep as Image Taken).

8. Once all these settings are selected, press MENU to turn off the menu screen.

9. A message will come on screen prompting you to take a test shot. Press OK. Take a test shot (or two) to make sure the settings give you correct focus and exposure.

10. Press the Movie Shooting button, then press the Shutter button to start shooting the time-lapse movie.

06 TYPICAL SHOOTING SCENARIOS

SHOOTING SCENARIO
PORTRAIT

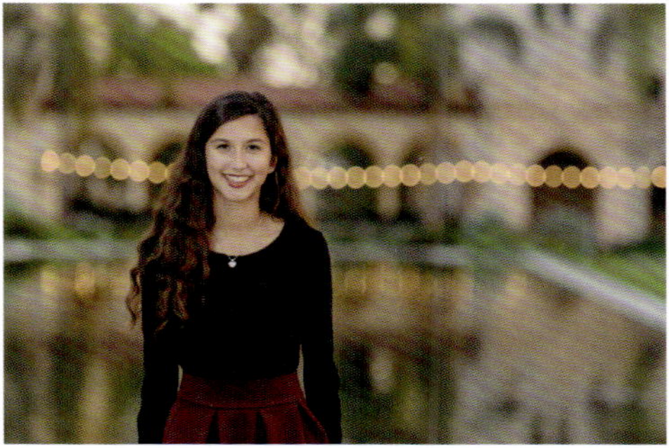

KEY PRINCIPLES

- The key to a portrait like this is shallow depth of field. So shoot in **APERTURE PRIORITY (Av)** mode and start with the lowest aperture your lens offers (such as **f/2.8 or f/4**).
- Remember to **focus on the eyes**.

- If the image is too dark or too light, use **EXPOSURE COMPENSATION** to adjust the brightness level.
- If the image is blurry from a slow shutter speed, **raise the ISO** to increase your sensor's sensitivity to light, thus allowing for a faster shutter speed.
- Remember to use a **focal length of 50mm or greater** so that you don't distort your subject's face.

SHOOTING SCENARIO
GROUP PORTRAIT

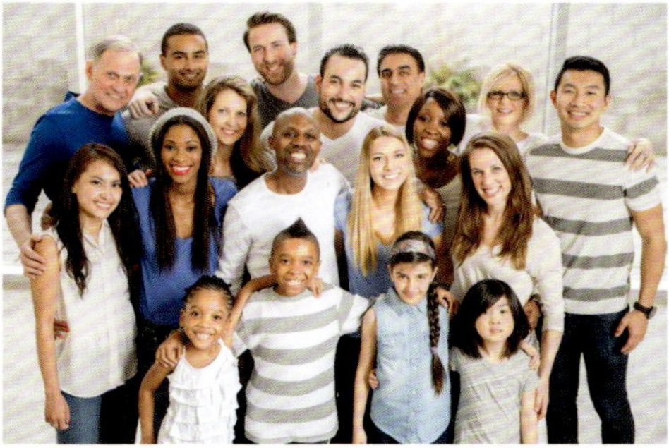

KEY PRINCIPLES

- In order to get everyone in focus, you need a deep depth of field. So shoot in **APERTURE PRIORITY (Av)** mode and set the aperture between **f/8–f/16**.
- **Focus on the person in the middle of the group**. Check the focus by using the LCD screen. View it at 100% and check faces in the front and back rows. If anyone is out of focus, use a smaller aperture for deeper depth of field.
- Use **EVALUATIVE METERING** to account for the light in the entire scene.
- **Arrange the group so they can all see you** (and you can see them).
- Use **EXPOSURE COMPENSATION** if the image is too bright or too dark.
- If image is blurry, **raise the ISO** to allow the camera to use a faster shutter speed.

SHOOTING SCENARIO

LANDSCAPE

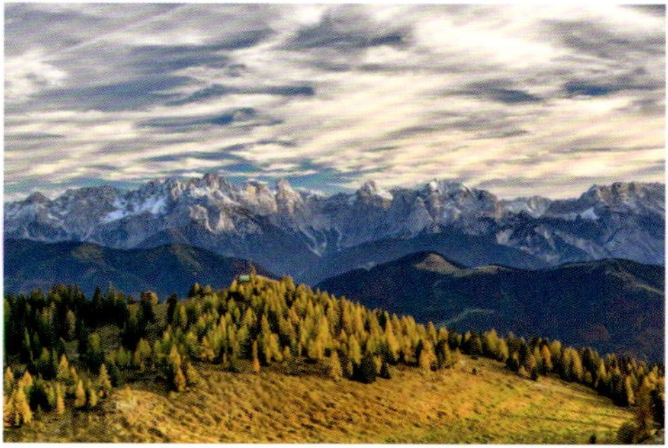

KEY PRINCIPLES

- Shoot in **APERTURE PRIORITY (Av) mode** to control depth of field, and start with **f/16** to ensure deep depth of field.
- **Use a tripod** to eliminate camera movement. Whenever your camera is on a tripod, also make sure that any **IMAGE STABILIZATION** is turned off.
- Use **EVALUATIVE METERING** and **ONE-SHOT AF** focus mode.
- **Set the ISO to a low setting (100–200)** to avoid any digital noise.

- Shoot in **RAW** so that you have the most available information when editing later.
- Consider **BRACKETING** your exposures.

SHOOTING SCENARIO
FREEZE ACTION

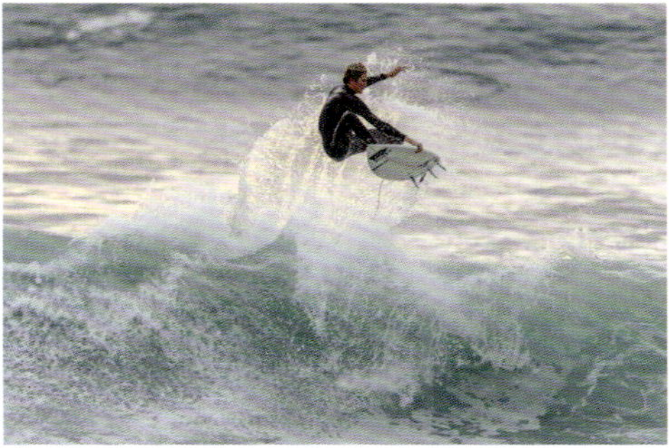

KEY PRINCIPLES

- Use **SHUTTER PRIORITY (Tv)** mode and set the shutter speed to a value that will freeze the action. The appropriate shutter speed depends on your subject and its movement, but could be anywhere between **1/500–1/8000 sec**.

- Use **SERVO** autofocus so that the camera keeps focusing as the subject moves.
- If the image is dark or blurry, **raise the ISO** or try AUTO ISO to automatically have the camera adjust the ISO as needed.

SHOOTING SCENARIO
SHOWING MOTION—PANNING

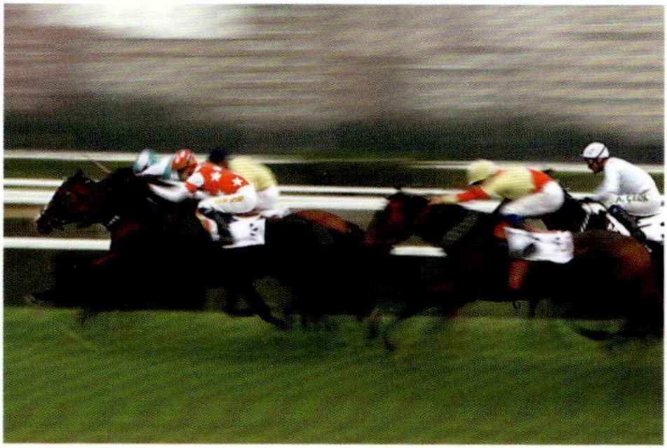

KEY PRINCIPLES

- Shoot in **SHUTTER PRIORITY (Tv)** mode and use a slow-enough shutter speed to allow for the subject to move during the exposure.

- **Follow the subject** across the frame as you shoot.
- Use **SERVO** autofocus, as well as the **EXPAND AF AREA** focus mode to ensure the camera focuses on the subject.

SHOOTING SCENARIO
LOW-LIGHT ACTION

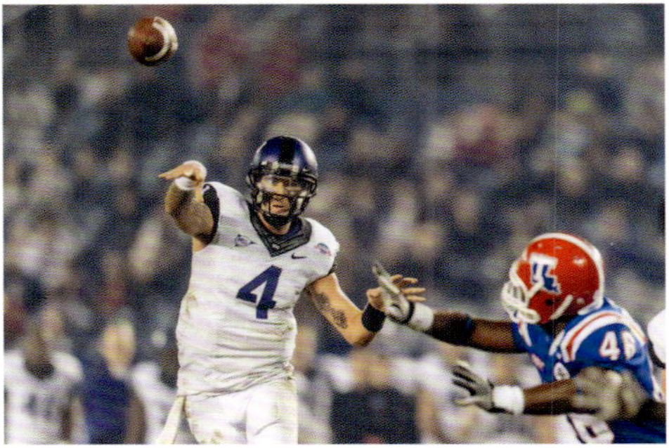

KEY PRINCIPLES

- Shoot in **APERTURE PRIORITY (Av)** mode and use a wide aperture such as **f/2.8 or f/4**.
- Use **PARTIAL METERING** and meter on the subject's face.
- Use **SERVO** autofocus and **1-POINT AF** (a single focus point).

- **Set the ISO to 1600 or higher**, depending on the amount of available light.
- If the image is blurry, **increase the ISO** to allow for a faster shutter speed.

SHOOTING SCENARIO
LONG EXPOSURE

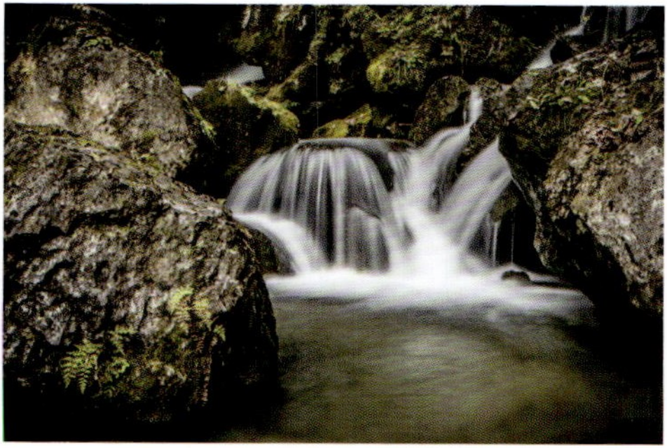

KEY PRINCIPLES

- Use **MANUAL** or **BULB** shooting mode so you can use a long shutter speed.
- **Use a tripod** to keep the camera stable. **Turn off any IMAGE STABILIZATION**.

- Use the **ONE-SHOT AF** focus mode, or try manual focus if the camera is having a hard time locking on focus.
- **Use a low ISO** (100–400) and **shoot RAW** to ensure a high-quality file.
- Use a **cable release** with a lock to avoid touching (shaking) the camera.

SHOOTING SCENARIO
MACRO/CLOSE-UP

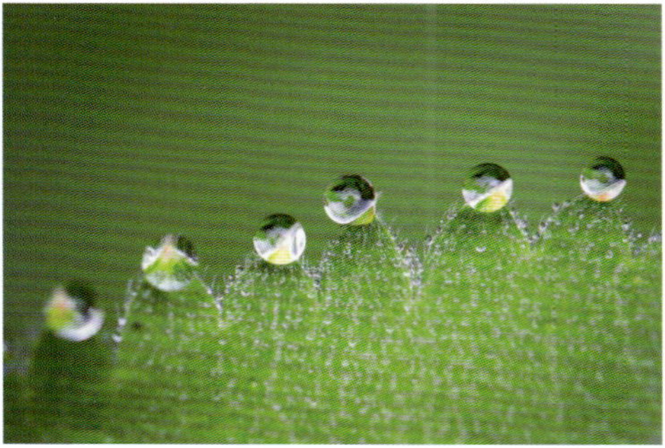

KEY PRINCIPLES

- Shoot in **APERTURE PRIORITY (Av)** mode and **use a small aperture** to ensure you achieve enough depth of field (this image was shot at f/13).
- Use **EVALUATIVE METERING** to analyze the light in the entire frame.
- A **tripod** is very useful for keeping the camera steady.
- Use **MANUAL FOCUS** and **zoom in** to confirm your focus is tack-sharp.
- Try using a dedicated **macro lens** or **close-up filters** to make sure you can achieve sharp focus when you're so close to the subject.

SHOOTING SCENARIO

VIDEO RECORDING/VLOGGING

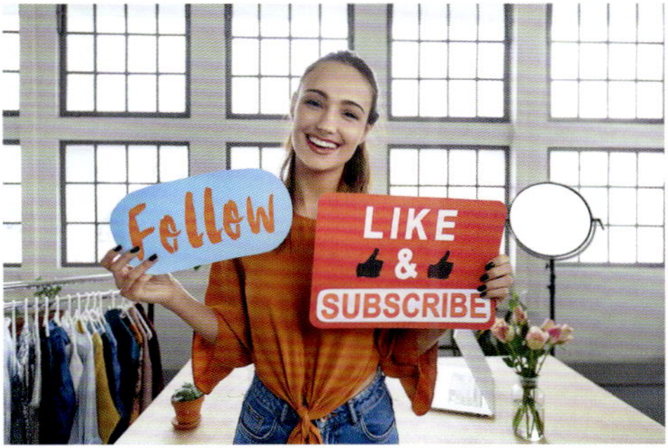

KEY PRINCIPLES

- Use a **shallow depth of field** to keep the viewers' attention on the subject. A **wide aperture** will keep the subject in focus while having the area in front of and behind the subject fall out of focus.
- Consider using **23.98 fps** for a more cinematic look. This is selected in MENU > Shooting (Screen 1) > Movie Recording Size.

- Try setting the **shutter speed** to **twice the frame rate**, or as close as you can get. If using 23.98 fps, the shutter speed should be 1/50 (or 1/60) second.
- Consider using an **external microphone** for better sound. For example, Canon makes the DM-E100 or the DM-E1, both of which are compatible with the R8.
- Keep the camera stable with a **tripod or gimble**. Smooth footage looks more professional.
- Remember to leave a second or two of empty footage at the beginning and end of your video clips, making them much easier to edit later.